THOUGHTS...

WHISPERS OF THE SOUL...

PRATYUSH MUDRA

Made with ♥ on the Notion Press Platform
www.notionpress.com

Dedication

To those who **dare** to **dream and feel** deeply, this collection is dedicated to **you**. May the whispers of the soul resonate within your heart, guiding you through the **labyrinth of emotions** and thoughts that shape our existence. To my family and friends, whose unwavering support and love have been my greatest inspiration; to the quiet moments that spark creativity; and to every reader who finds solace in these verses—this book is for **you**. May it serve as a gentle reminder that **we are all connected** by the threads of our shared experiences, and may you always **find beauty in the whispers** that surround you.

Contents

Contents

Contents

Contents

Contents

Foreword

Welcome to my **debut poetry collection**! My name is **Pratyush Mudra**, and I am excited to share this journey of **self-discovery** and **expression** with you. As a student navigating the complexities of life, I have found **solace and clarity** in the art of poetry. Each poem in this collection reflects my **thoughts**, **emotions**, and **experiences**, capturing the essence of my journey so far. Through these verses, I hope to **connect with you**, evoking feelings that **resonate and inspire**. Thank you for joining me on this adventure; your support means the world to me as I take my first steps into the **realm of poetry** publishing.

Preface

Welcome to "**Thoughts: Whispers of the Soul**," a collection that invites you into the **intimate corners** of my mind and heart. This book is a reflection of my journey through life's complexities, emotions, and revelations. Each poem serves as a **whisper**, capturing **fleeting moments of joy**, **sorrow**, **love**, and **introspection**. As you turn these pages, I hope you find echoes of your own experiences and emotions, creating a shared connection between us. Poetry has always been my **refuge**, a means to **articulate** the **inexpressible**, and I am thrilled to share this part of my soul with you. Thank you for joining me on this **exploration of thought and feeling**; may these verses resonate with you and inspire **your own whispers**.

Acknowledgements

In the creation of "**Thoughts: Whispers of the Soul**," I am deeply grateful to everyone who has **accompanied** me on this journey. To my family and friends, your unwavering support and encouragement have been my **guiding light**, inspiring me to **delve** into the depths of my emotions and share my truth. To my **mentors** and **fellow writers**, thank you for your invaluable insights and for **fostering** a community where creativity can **flourish**. Lastly, to the readers who take the time to engage with these pages, your **willingness to explore** the **whispers of my soul** means the world to me. This book is a **reflection** of our shared **humanity**, and I **hope** it resonates with you as **profoundly** as it has with me.

Prologue

In the **quiet moments** between **waking** and **dreaming**, where thoughts **drift** like leaves on a **gentle stream**, lies the **essence** of the soul's whisper. *"**Thoughts: Whispers of the Soul**"* is a journey through this **serene landscape**—a collection of verses that seeks to capture the **delicate echoes** of our **innermostmusings**.

This book is not merely a compilation of poems; it is a **reflection of the human spirit**, a **tapestry** woven from threads of **introspection**, **emotion**, and **experience**. Each poem is a fragment of a larger conversation with the self, a dialogue between the heart and mind that resonates with the universal quest for **meaning** and **connection**.

In these pages, you will find the **subtleties** of life's quiet moments, the **profound in the ordinary**, and the **beauty** that often goes unnoticed. These whispers are invitations—to pause, to reflect, and to find solace in the shared experience of being.

May these words **accompany** you on your own journey, offering **glimpses** of **understanding** and **comfort**. As you turn each page, I hope you find a **mirror** to your own thoughts and a **companion** in your **quest for deeper truths**.

Welcome to this **exploration of the soul's whispers**.

—**Pratyush Mudra**

CLASSIC THOUGHTS...

1. The Echoing Hall

Within a hall of echoes grand,
Where every sound reverberates,
The whispers of the ages stand,
In timeless, soft debates.
The walls are lined with history,
In every creak and gentle moan,
The hall becomes a mystery,
Of voices that are softly known.
In this space, where echoes dwell,
The past and present gently meet,
In every sound, a story tells,
A rhythm, calm and sweet.
So wander through this hallowed space,
Let the echoes guide your mind,
In their resonance, find grace,
And leave your worries far behind.

2. The Lantern's Glow

In the stillness of the night,
When shadows cloak the world in peace,
A lantern casts a gentle light,
And whispers soft as stars release.
Its glow, a beacon through the dark,
Guides lost souls with tender flare,
A symbol of a hopeful spark,
In moments filled with silent care.
The lantern's flame, a quiet guide,
Through journeys of the heart and mind,
Its light will never falter, hide,
But shine with warmth that's intertwined.
In its soft and steady beam,
Find solace in the quiet night,
A promise of a hopeful dream,
Within its gentle, glowing light.
So let the lantern's light embrace,
Your spirit as you wander on,
In its glow, find your own place,
And let your fears and doubts be gone.

3. The Whispering Sea

By the shore where waves caress,
The sea whispers secrets old,
In every tide, a soft address,
Of tales the ocean has retold.
The surf, a constant, rolling song,
It speaks of lands both far and near,
Its rhythm, steady and strong,
Carries echoes we can hear.
The sea's embrace is vast and wide,
Its whispers blend with salt and air,
In its depths, where dreams reside,
The soul finds solace, sweet and rare.
So listen to the ocean's breath,
Let its rhythm soothe your soul,
In its whispers, find a depth,
Where dreams and peace are whole.

4. The Forgotten Fountain

In a garden cloaked in moss and time,
Where a fountain's song is faint,
The water whispers in its chime,
A tale of old, both sweet and quaint.
The stone is worn, the edges blurred,
Yet still, it holds a silent grace,
In every drop, a vision stirred,
Of days long past and their embrace.
The fountain's song is soft and clear,
A melody of ancient lore,
It speaks of love and joy sincere,
Of dreams that linger evermore.
In the stillness, hear its call,
A gentle hymn to times gone by,
The fountain's voice will gently fall,
As echoes of the past float by.
So pause and listen to its song,
Let it soothe your weary soul,
In its whispers, find where you belong,
In the timeless, ageless role.

5. The Moonlight Love

In the quite night where light softly gleams,
The sun and moon dance in gentle streams,
He brings the warmth, she bring the glow,
A love story that all the heavens know.
With fiery rays, he paints the day,
She weaves soft light in the night's display,
Together they weave a tapestry bright,
A love that shines through day and night.
At dawn, he bids farewell with a gentle kiss,
She rises quitely in the morning bliss,
Their bond unbreakable, their love so true,
In the moonlight sky, a romance anew.
For when he sleeps, she lights the way,
A love eternal, come what may,
In every phase, in every arc above,
Their dance continues, in Moonlight Love.

6. The Whispering Wind

In the hush of twilight's sigh,
The wind begins its whispered tale,
Through leaves and branches, soft and shy,
It weaves a story without fail.
The breeze, a keeper of the past,
It carries voices, faint and clear,
Through ages long and shadows cast,
It speaks to hearts that choose to hear.
In every gust, a secret lies,
Of moments lost and days gone by,
The wind's soft murmur, like a prize,
Brings memories beneath the sky.
Its whispers float on evening's breath,
A serenade to those who listen,
In its song, there's life and death,
And dreams that softly glisten.
So let the whispering wind entwine
With your thoughts as day departs,
In its gentle, soothing line,
Find echoes of your heart.

7. The Timeworn Path

Upon a timeworn, winding path,
Where footsteps echo soft and clear,
The road reveals its ancient wrath,
And whispers of the bygone year.
Each stone and turn holds tales of yore,
Of journeys made and hearts once bold,
The path retains its timeless lore,
In stories subtly told.
The trees that arch above this way,
Stand guardian to years gone past,
Their branches weave a canopy,
Where memories and dreams are cast.
In the quiet of this trail,
The past and present intertwine,
Each step reveals a faint detail,
A glimpse of what was once divine.
So tread this path with reverent care,
Let each stride become a song,
For in its echoes, softly bare,
The soul and time are ever strong.

8. The Silent Meadows

In meadows where the wildflowers sway,
Where nature's palette gently blends,
The silence speaks in its own way,
A quiet song that never ends.
The grasses whisper to the breeze,
Their secrets shared in soft, green tones,
In every rustle through the trees,
The meadow's heart is gently known.
The sun dips low, a golden sweep,
Across the fields where shadows play,
The day drifts by in tranquil sleep,
And twilight greets the coming gray.
In this serene, untouched expanse,
The soul can find a space to dream,
In nature's calm, a fleeting glance,
At life's most subtle, gentle scheme.
So rest within this quiet land,
Let the meadows soothe your soul,
In their silence, take a stand,
And let your spirit find its goal.

9. The Morning's Caress

As dawn unveils its tender light,
The world awakens soft and slow,
In hues of gold and gentle white,
The morning's touch begins to show.
The whispers of the night retreat,
As sunlight warms the dewy earth,
In every ray, a promise sweet,
Of daybreak's calm and quiet mirth.
The birds converse in melodies,
Their songs a balm to weary hearts,
In morning's hush, the soul finds ease,
As new beginnings gently start.
Each moment sparkles in the light,
A chance to breathe, to start anew,
In the morning's soft embrace,
Find peace in every shade and hue.
So greet the day with open arms,
Let morning's caress soothe your mind,
In its embrace, discover charms,
And leave the shadows far behind.

10. The Whisper of Time

In the quiet of an ancient hall,
Where shadows linger, soft and deep,
The whispers of the ages call,
In echoes where the past does sleep.
Each corner holds a fleeting trace,
Of moments that have drifted by,
The walls remember every face,
And time's refrain is soft and shy.
The tapestry of days unfurls,
In patterns worn with age and grace,
A story in each thread that swirls,
Of lives and dreams and their embrace.
Listen to the silent song,
The whisper of the years gone past,
In its cadence, find where you belong,
A harmony that's meant to last.
So wander through this timeworn space,
Let the echoes guide your thought,
In every whisper, find a place,
Where memories and dreams are caught.

IMAGINARY THOUGHTS...

11. The Land Of Echoes

In the land where echoes softly play,
Dreams unfold in twilight's sway,
Whispers drift on moonlit streams,
And shadows dance with fleeting dreams.
Mountains rise from misty veils,
Casting tales in whispered trails,
Valleys hum with secrets old,
In the land of thoughts untold.
Stars weave patterns in the night,
Guiding thoughts with gentle light,
Constellations, tales of yore,
Paint the sky with myths and lore.
Breezes carry songs of grace,
Sculpting forms in endless space,
Echoes form in twilight's breath,
A tapestry of life and death.
As dawn breaks, the echoes fade,
Yet their whispers never jade,
In the heart, the dreams remain,
A land where echoes leave their stain.

12. The Dreamsmith's Forge

In a forge where dreams are made,
The dreamsmith's hands with fire played,
Crafting thoughts from molten night,
Forging visions pure and bright.
Anvil rings with rhythmic might,
Hammer shapes the darkened light,
Stars are quenched in twilight's hue,
Crafting dreams both old and new.
Celestial sparks and ember trails,
Turn to visions, grand details,
Moonlight dances in the flame,
Shaping dreams with whispered names.
Each creation, a work of art,
Carved from the depths of the heart,
As dawn approaches, dreams take flight,
Forged by the smith of endless night.

13. The Secret of the Stars

Beyond the veil of night's embrace,
A secret lies in starry space,
Whispers of the cosmos call,
Through the night, a soft enthrall.
Galaxies in distant dance,
Spin their tales in cosmic trance,
Nebulae of colors blend,
In the silence, dreams ascend.
Each twinkle holds a story true,
Of ancient realms and skies anew,
Constellations softly weave,
Patterns only night can conceive.
In the hush of starlit skies,
The soul finds wonder and replies,
For in each star's eternal gleam,
Resides the essence of a dream.

14. The Celestial Garden

In gardens where the stardust grows,
Where moonlight falls on velvet leaves,
There blooms a realm where magic flows,
And every thought a dream retrieves.
The petals glow with cosmic hues,
A fusion of the night and day,
And in their light, the mind can choose,
To wander where the shadows play.
The fragrance is a whispered tale,
Of galaxies and stars entwined,
And every breeze a secret frail,
Of dreams and thoughts that wander blind.
The pathways in this garden shine,
With every step a soft surprise,
Where every star and leaf align,
To weave the wonders of the skies.
So roam amidst this dreamlike space,
Where stardust dances in your wake,
And let the beauty of this place,
Inspire thoughts that softly quake.

15. The Invisible Kingdom

Beyond the veil where shadows drift,
A kingdom forms in silent grace,
Where dreams and thoughts in whispers lift,
And time and space begin to chase.
The castles float on phantom streams,
With towers reaching through the mist,
And in their halls, the midnight dreams,
Are woven in a twilight twist.
The courtiers in their spectral gowns,
Are draped in shades of moonlit gold,
Their voices soft in haunting tones,
Speak tales of dreams both young and old.
The land is draped in twilight's hue,
Where echoes of the past convene,
And every path a journey new,
Through realms where only thoughts have been.
So enter this ethereal domain,
Where dreams and shadows intertwine,
And find within the phantom rain,
The kingdom where your thoughts align.

16. The Dream Weaver

In chambers where the twilight spins,
A dream weaver crafts her art,
With threads of silver, soft as sins,
She weaves the dreams of every heart.
The loom is set with starlit strands,
And every thread a whisper brings,
Of dreams that drift to distant lands,
Where moonlight softly spreads its wings.
The patterns form in mystic dance,
With every shift, a tale is spun,
Of realms where night and dreams enhance,
And time itself becomes undone.
The tapestry of dreams reveals,
The hidden thoughts and wishes bright,
And in its fabric, truth conceals,
The essence of the endless night.
So close your eyes and let the weave,
Of dreams and stardust gently hold,
For in the patterns, you'll perceive,
The stories of the night unfold.

17. The Ethereal Circus

In twilight's hush, the circus blooms,
With stars as tents and dreams as games,
Where moonlight paints the velvet rooms,
And every act a soft acclaim.
The acrobats in stardust glide,
Their movements light as midnight air,
And in their dance, the dreams reside,
A wonderment beyond compare.
The clowns are draped in spectral hues,
Their laughter soft as evening's call,
And every jest and trick imbues,
A magic that the night installs.
The ringmaster's voice, a gentle song,
Guides every dream through cosmic rings,
And in his words, the realms belong,
To the tales the night sky brings.
So join this dreamscape, soft and bright,
Where every star and circus play,
And let your thoughts take wing tonight,
In realms where dreams and nightbirds sway.

18. The Whispering Forest

In forests where the twilight weaves,
A realm of whispers softly calls,
Where shadows dance between the leaves,
And every thought in silence falls.
The trees are cloaked in moonlit grace,
Their branches sway with secrets old,
And every breeze a soft embrace,
Of dreams and tales that night foretold.
The paths are lined with stardust bright,
Where echoes of the past entwine,
And every step a dance of light,
Through realms where moon and dreams align.
The forest hums a mystic song,
With melodies of hidden lore,
And in its depths, the dreams belong,
To those who seek and evermore.
So wander through this twilight space,
Where whispers guide the heart's delight,
And find within the forest's face,
The dreams that gently greet the night.

19. The Phantom Lighthouse

Upon the shore of phantom seas,
Where moonlight casts its silver spell,
There stands a lighthouse in the breeze,
With dreams and thoughts its beacons tell.
The light that sweeps across the waves,
Is not of lanterns bright and warm,
But of the dreams that time engraves,
In patterns soft, a gentle charm.
The beams that pierce the midnight air,
Are whispers of the past's embrace,
And in their light, the heart can dare,
To seek the dreams beyond their space.
The keeper of this spectral light,
Is shadowed in the misty deep,
And in his gaze, the dreams take flight,
To places where the phantoms sleep.
So follow where the light may lead,
And let the dreams of night unfold,
For in the beacon's silent heed,
You'll find the stories soft and bold.

20. The Enchanted Observatory

In towers where the starlight pools,
An observatory of dreams stands,
Where every thought and night unfolds,
In cosmic maps and stardust bands.
The telescope of silvered glass,
Reveals the realms where dreams take flight,
And through its lens, the visions pass,
Of worlds beyond the darkened night.
The charts are inked with cosmic lore,
And every line a whispered tale,
Of lands where dreams and stars explore,
And fantasy and truth unveil.
The constellations gently sing,
A symphony of dreams and light,
And in their harmonies, you'll cling,
To visions of the endless night.
So gaze into the starlit view,
And let the universe inspire,
For in the observatory's cue,
The dreams and thoughts of night conspire.

HEALING THOUGHTS...

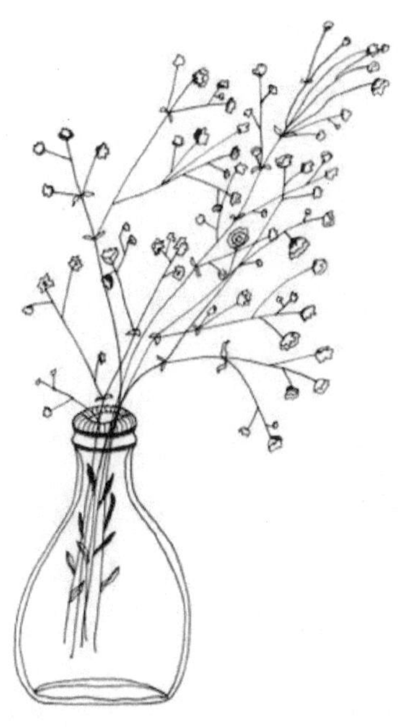

21. The Gentle Embrace

In twilight's calm, where shadows rest,
A gentle breath of peace descends,
The heart begins its tender quest,
To heal where every sorrow mends.
The softest whispers of the night,
Are balm to wounds both deep and small,
In moonlit dreams, we find the light,
And in its glow, we start to fall.
The echoes of our deepest fears,
Are soothed by time's unhurried grace,
And in the stillness of the years,
We find the strength to reembrace.
Each dawn brings forth a healing song,
A melody of hope anew,
Where once we felt that we were wrong,
We find a path, both bright and true.
So let the whispers gently guide,
Your heart to places warm and whole,
For in the night where thoughts reside,
You'll find the peace that heals the soul.

22. The River of Renewal

Beneath the sky's expansive blue,
A river flows with healing grace,
Its waters clear, a tranquil view,
Reflect the peace of a calm place.
The currents carry dreams away,
And wash the wounds of yesterday,
With every ripple, fears decay,
And in their place, new hopes will stay.
The river sings a soothing tune,
Of past and future intertwined,
Its melody beneath the moon,
Unfolds the strength that's redefined.
The flow of time, both pure and wide,
Brings healing in its gentle stream,
And in its course, we'll safely glide,
To find the peace within our dream.
So let the river's whispers call,
And guide your heart through healing tides,
For in its depths, you'll find the fall,
Of troubles where serenity hides.

23. The Garden of Solace

In gardens where the lilies bloom,
Where sunlight dances on the leaves,
There lies a realm devoid of gloom,
Where every heartache gently cleaves.
The petals soft with morning dew,
Embrace the wounds of restless hearts,
And in their touch, the spirits renew,
As healing in their presence starts.
The fragrance of the blooming wild,
Carries peace on gentle breeze,
And in its scent, the soul's beguiled,
To find the calm that never flees.
The colors blend in vibrant hues,
A tapestry of hope and grace,
And in this garden, every muse,
Finds solace in its tender space.
So wander through this healing field,
Where every flower sings a song,
And let your heart begin to yield,
To peace where you have longed so long.

24. The Dawn of Forgiveness

With dawn's first light, the shadows fade,
And healing whispers softly call,
A new beginning gently made,
Where past and future intertwine, enthrall.
The morning's glow, a tender kiss,
Unfolds the wounds of yesterday,
And in its warmth, there's gentle bliss,
A promise that the heart can sway.
Forgiveness like the rising sun,
Dispels the night of hurt and pain,
And with its light, the healing's done,
A soothing balm for every strain.
The day unfolds with gentle grace,
And in its light, the soul finds rest,
For in this dawn, you'll find your place,
And heal the wounds that once oppressed.
So let the dawn embrace your soul,
And with its grace, your heart release,
For in this light, you'll find the whole,
Of healing thoughts and inner peace.

25. The Silent Sanctuary

In spaces where the silence breathes,
A sanctuary softly grows,
Where healing thought and calm conceives,
And every heartache gently goes.
The quiet hums a soothing tune,
That calms the tempest of the mind,
And in its peace, the soul's attuned,
To every thought that's kind and kind.
The walls are draped in gentle hue,
A palette of the softest shades,
And in this place where spirits strew,
The burdens of the heart cascades.
The silence holds a tender grace,
A refuge from the world's loud clamor,
Where every thought finds its own place,
And healing comes without a hammer.
So seek this refuge, soft and still,
Where silence heals and thoughts are clear,
For in this space, the heart can will,
A peace that's felt and deeply near.

26. The Healing Rain

When clouds release their tender tears,
And rain begins its gentle fall,
The earth receives with open ears,
A soothing gift that heals us all.
The droplets kiss the parched earth's skin,
And cleanse away the dust of time,
And in their touch, the life begins,
To blossom forth in purest rhyme.
The storm, though fierce, brings forth new growth,
And in its strength, we find our grace,
For every drop, a promise both,
Of healing in its soft embrace.
The rain renews the soul's own song,
With every drop, a gentle balm,
And in its rhythm, we belong,
To peace and dreams both kind and calm.
So let the rain wash through your soul,
And in its rhythm find the balm,
For in its song, you'll find the whole,
Of peace and hope that's soft and calm.

27. The Embrace of Time

In the arms of patient time,
Where moments weave a tapestry,
There lies a space both soft and kind,
Where healing thoughts begin to be.
The hours drift in gentle sway,
Their passing soothes the restless heart,
And in their flow, the pain gives way,
To peace where every wound can start.
The days unfold in softest hues,
A canvas for the soul's retreat,
And in their light, the mind renews,
And finds the strength to be complete.
The seasons turn with patient grace,
And in their cycles, healing lies,
A steady rhythm, soft embrace,
That brings the peace beneath the skies.
So let the hands of time embrace,
Your weary heart and restless mind,
For in its grace, you'll find a place,
Where healing thoughts are gently kind.

28. The Lantern's Light

In the hush of night's embrace,
A lantern glows with healing grace,
Its light a beacon through the dark,
To guide the soul and leave its mark.
The flicker dances soft and slow,
A rhythm of the heart's relief,
And in its warmth, the shadows go,
Replaced by peace and tender belief.
The lantern's light is ever true,
A symbol of the heart's own quest,
To find the calm that lies within,
And grant the spirit gentle rest.
Its glow can mend the deepest pain,
And light the path to hope anew,
For in its beams, the soul will gain,
The strength to find what's kind and true.
So hold the lantern close and dear,
And let its light dispel the gloom,
For in its glow, you'll find the clear,
Of healing thoughts in every room.

29. The Woven Threads

In the loom of night's soft grace,
The threads of healing gently weave,
A fabric of a tranquil space,
Where wounds and fears begin to leave.
Each thread a whisper of the past,
And every weave a gentle mend,
The tapestry of peace is cast,
In patterns that the heart will blend.
The colors blend in soothing swirls,
A symphony of calm and light,
And in its weave, the pain unfurls,
Replaced by thoughts that softly ignite.
The fabric tells of journeys long,
Of trials faced and peace embraced,
And in its warmth, you'll find the song,
Of healing thoughts in every place.
So let the loom of night embrace,
The heart and spirit, soft and whole,
For in its threads, you'll find the space,
Where healing thoughts renew the soul.

30. The Path of Light

On paths where dawn and twilight meet,
A journey of the soul begins,
Where healing light and shadows greet,
And every step a new hope wins.
The path is paved with golden rays,
That guide the heart through every strife,
And in their light, the spirit sways,
To find the peace that ends the strife.
The journey's end is not a place,
But in the heart where dreams reside,
And every step a gentle grace,
That leads the soul to soft abide.
The light will lead through dark and shade,
And show the way to hope and cheer,
For in its glow, the heart is made,
To heal and find the path so clear.
So walk the path where light extends,
And let its glow your spirit find,
For in its warmth, the heart will mend,
And healing thoughts will ease the mind.

ETERNAL THOUGHTS...

31. Timeless Echoes

In ancient halls where whispers dwell,
Eternal thoughts in shadows play,
Their echoes through the ages swell,
And weave the fabric of today.
The stars above in silent grace,
Reflect the dreams of those long gone,
Their light a timeless, soft embrace,
That guides the heart from dusk to dawn.
The sands of time, in endless flow,
Reveal the patterns of our quest,
And in their grains, the stories grow,
Of dreams and thoughts that never rest.
The cosmos holds a boundless space,
For every thought that's ever known,
And in its vast and endless grace,
The seeds of wisdom softly sown.
So let the echoes gently guide,
Your soul through realms of endless night,
For in their whispers, deep and wide,
You'll find the path to timeless light.

32. Eternal Reverie

In dreams that dance beyond the day,
Eternal thoughts begin their flight,
They linger where the shadows play,
And paint the canvas of the night.
The moonlight casts a silver veil,
On landscapes of the mind's domain,
Where every thought is soft and frail,
Yet echoes through the vast terrain.
The tides of time in rhythmic sweep,
Carry visions far and wide,
And in their currents, we shall keep,
The dreams that on the waves reside.
The stars align in patterns grand,
A map of endless, cosmic lore,
And in their glow, we understand,
The truths that thoughts forever store.
So drift upon this reverie,
Where timeless wonders softly gleam,
For in this space, you'll come to see,
The essence of the eternal dream.

33. The Eternal Flame

In the hearth of endless night,
An eternal flame does burn,
Its light a beacon pure and bright,
For every soul that seeks to learn.
The fire's glow is soft yet strong,
A guide through dark and shifting tides,
And in its warmth, the heart belongs,
To realms where timeless thought abides.
The embers hold the ancient lore,
Of ages past and futures near,
And in their light, we see once more,
The truths that thoughts forever clear.
The flame endures through every storm,
A symbol of the heart's own grace,
And in its light, the mind transforms,
To find its place in boundless space.
So tend this flame within your heart,
And let its light forever guide,
For in its warmth, you'll find the art,
Of thoughts that never fade or hide.

34. Whispers of Infinity

In the silence of the night,
Where stars and dreams in silence meet,
Eternal whispers take their flight,
On winds of time that never cheat.
The cosmos sings its ancient song,
Of worlds that spin in endless grace,
And in its music, we belong,
To realms that time cannot erase.
The galaxies in cosmic dance,
Reveal the threads of fate and chance,
And in their spins, our thoughts enhance,
To touch the realm of pure expanse.
The universe, a boundless sea,
Holds every thought in its embrace,
And in its depths, our souls are free,
To wander through the endless space.
So listen to infinity's call,
And let its whispers guide you through,
For in its depth, you'll find the all,
Of thoughts both old and ever new.

35. The Ageless Tree

In the garden where the ages blend,
An ageless tree stands tall and wise,
Its roots entwine where past and end,
And reach to touch the endless skies.
The branches spread in silent grace,
And hold the thoughts of every year,
Each leaf a page, a sacred place,
Where timeless truths appear so clear.
The seasons turn, the years unfold,
Yet still the tree remains the same,
Its wisdom in its bark is told,
A testament to life's great aim.
The roots delve deep in cosmic soil,
Where ancient memories reside,
And in its shade, our hearts recoil,
From transient woes to thoughts that bide.
So sit beneath this ageless tree,
And feel its wisdom calm and bright,
For in its presence, you will see,
The thoughts that dwell in endless light.

36. The Celestial Script

On parchment of the starlit sky,
The celestial script is penned,
With every star a dot and sigh,
Of thoughts that time cannot amend.
The constellations form the lines,
Of stories written long ago,
And in their glow, our hearts define,
The paths that we are meant to go.
The ink of night is deep and vast,
A canvas of the cosmic lore,
And in its folds, the present, past,
And future intertwine and soar.
The galaxies in distant sweep,
Compose the verses of our fate,
And in their dance, the secrets keep,
Of thoughts that time will not abate.
So read the script of heaven's quill,
And let its wisdom guide your soul,
For in its lines, you'll find the thrill,
Of thoughts that make the spirit whole.

37. The Infinite Horizon

On horizons where the sky meets sea,
Eternal thoughts in silence roam,
They stretch beyond what eyes can see,
To realms that time has yet to comb.
The waves of time roll soft and wide,
And carry dreams on every crest,
Where endless vistas open wide,
To show the thoughts that never rest.
The sunset paints a timeless hue,
That fades yet always stays in sight,
And in its colors, deep and true,
Are thoughts that guide us through the night.
The twilight whispers soft and slow,
Of journeys vast and realms unknown,
And in its light, the thoughts will show,
The paths to places we have grown.
So gaze upon this endless line,
Where sky and sea forever blend,
And in its vastness, you will find,
The thoughts that stretch beyond the end.

38. The Eternal Symphony

In the halls of cosmic sound,
An eternal symphony plays,
Its notes in timeless rhythm found,
Guide hearts through dark and fleeting days.
The melodies of ancient lore,
Resound in every breath and beat,
And through their strains, we come to know,
The thoughts that make existence sweet.
The orchestra of stars and light,
Performs the music of the spheres,
And in its grandeur, soft and bright,
The wisdom of the cosmos clears.
The harmony of night and dawn,
Blends thoughts of past with those to come,
And in its notes, the heart is drawn,
To rhythms that forever hum.
So listen to this ageless tune,
And let its music fill your soul,
For in its symphony's soft croon,
You'll find the thoughts that make you whole.

39. The Eternal Fountain

In a meadow where the waters gleam,
An eternal fountain flows,
Its crystal streams a boundless dream,
Where every thought in stillness grows.
The liquid light reflects the stars,
And carries wisdom through its tide,
With every drop, the soul departs,
To realms where timeless truths abide.
The fountain sings a song so old,
Of love and peace and dreams anew,
Its echoes through the ages told,
In waters clear and skies of blue.
The gentle flow, a soothing balm,
To every heart that seeks to find,
In its embrace, the healing calm,
Of thoughts that stretch beyond the mind.
So drink from this eternal spring,
And let its waters cleanse your soul,
For in its depths, you'll find the ring,
Of thoughts that make the spirit whole.

40. The Everlasting Star

In the vast and endless night,
A single star forever burns,
Its light a guide through dark and light,
Where every thought and dream returns.
The star stands timeless, bold and bright,
A beacon through the cosmic sea,
And in its glow, the heart takes flight,
To realms where thoughts are ever free.
Its brilliance paints the heavens wide,
With stories of the age-long quest,
And in its light, the soul confides,
In dreams and hopes that never rest.
The star's eternal flame of gold,
Reminds us of the paths we tread,
And in its warmth, the truths unfold,
Of thoughts that time has never shed.
So gaze upon this endless star,
And let its light your spirit guide,
For in its glow, you'll find afar,
The thoughts that through the ages bide.

NEVER ENDING THOUGHTS...

41. Echoes in the Void

In quiet corners, whispers play,
Thoughts like echoes drift away.
In shadows deep where dreams reside,
They wander on with time's own tide.
Fragments drift on currents wide,
Lost within the mind's own tide.
Unspoken truths and silent calls,
In endless void where silence falls.
Waves of wonder rise and break,
In the depths where echoes wake.
Time dissolves in endless space,
Thoughts are found in darkened place.
Through the night, these whispers wend,
In the chasms where they blend.
Endless echoes softly call,
In the silence, they enthrall.
As dawn's light begins to show,
Thoughts retreat but do not go.
Come the night, they'll rise anew,
Endless echoes, fresh and true.

42. The Infinite Mirror

A mirror vast, reflecting time,
Shows the past and future's climb.
In each glance, new worlds appear,
Endless scenes are always near.
Reflections spin in endless play,
A dance of light in shadowed gray.
Every image tells a tale,
In the mirror's endless scale.
Time becomes a fleeting shade,
In this realm where thoughts cascade.
Mirrors of the mind unfold,
Stories whispered, truths retold.
Faces shift and intertwine,
In the glass where thoughts align.
Every glance reveals anew,
A universe both old and true.
In the mirror, dreams expand,
Thoughts forever, unplanned.
Endless orbs of light and grace,
In the reflections' endless space.

43. The Eternal Stream

In the river where thoughts flow,
Endless currents softly grow.
Ripples tell of tales unknown,
In the stream where dreams are sown.
Waves of wonder gently rise,
In the depths where silence lies.
Thoughts like fish swim deep and clear,
In the waters ever near.
Endless motion, no fixed shore,
In the stream, thoughts evermore.
Flowing through the mind's own sea,
Carrying dreams so wild and free.
In the quiet depths below,
Thoughts meander, softly glow.
The river whispers, never ends,
In the stream where time transcends.
As currents shift and softly play,
Thoughts continue on their way.
In the endless, flowing stream,
Thoughts and dreams forever gleam.

44. The Perpetual Dance

Thoughts like dancers in the night,
Twirl and spin in soft moonlight.
In a ballroom, shadows gleam,
Waltzing through a timeless dream.
Every step a fleeting rhyme,
Marking moments, passing time.
Their movement is a graceful trance,
In the endless, moonlit dance.
Pairs of memories gently sway,
In the dance of night and day.
Each turn a story old and new,
In the steps where thoughts pursue.
With each movement, rhythms play,
In the dance of night and day.
No final bow, no end in sight,
Just the dance of endless night.
As the dancers twirl and spin,
Thoughts take flight, both out and in.
In the dance of endless grace,
Thoughts find their sacred place.

45. The Whispering Labyrinth

A labyrinth within the mind,
Where winding paths are intertwined.
Each turn reveals a thought's embrace,
In the maze of dreams and space.
Walls of memory rise and fall,
In this endless, echoing hall.
Passages twist and shadows play,
In the silent, darkened sway.
Every corner holds a clue,
Silent whispers, old and new.
In this maze of shifting lore,
Thoughts forever seek and soar.
At the center, truths concealed,
In the heart of this mystic field.
Endless paths and shifting light,
Guide the mind through endless night.
In the labyrinth's endless maze,
Thoughts continue in their ways.
Lost and found, yet always near,
In the whispering hall of fear.

46. The Celestial Orbs

Stars above in endless space,
Glimmer softly, leave a trace.
Thoughts like orbs in cosmic sea,
Drift and swirl eternally.
Galaxies spin, vast and wide,
In the cosmos where dreams abide.
Each star a spark of ancient lore,
In the heavens' gentle roar.
Constellations weave their tales,
In the night where thought prevails.
Nebulae of dreams expand,
In this vast, celestial land.
As stars ignite and gently fade,
Thoughts persist in darkened shade.
In the sky of endless view,
Thoughts and dreams are born anew.
Though the night may shift and gleam,
Thoughts persist in boundless dream.
In the cosmic, endless flight,
Stars and thoughts burn bright through night.

47. The Unwritten Page

A blank page waits, serene and white,
For thoughts to fill with pure delight.
In emptiness, a boundless space,
Where stories find their timeless place.
Ink flows like a river's stream,
In the mind's vast, endless dream.
Words emerge and fade away,
On the page that holds the day.
Every line a path untold,
In the book where thoughts unfold.
A narrative twists and turns,
In the page where the soul yearns.
Though ink may smudge and blur anew,
New thoughts rise to fill the view.
The unwritten page remains,
A canvas where thought sustains.
With each thought that seeks to play,
The page renews with each new day.
In the cycle of the script,
Endless stories are equipped.

48. The Everlasting Flame

In the hearth where dreams ignite,
Burns a flame of endless light.
Thoughts are embers in the fire,
Flickering with deep desire.
Blazing trails of warmth and glow,
In the heart where passions flow.
Each spark a whisper, soft and bright,
In the flame's eternal light.
The fire dances, leaps, and bends,
In its warmth, the thought transcends.
Every crackle, tale unfolds,
In the blaze where passion holds.
Though the logs may turn to ash,
The flame endures, a constant flash.
In its light, thoughts burn so clear,
An everlasting, fiery sphere.
As the flame's embrace persists,
Thoughts are kindled, never missed.
In the heart where fires blaze,
Endless thoughts in fiery rays.

49. The Timeless Echo

In corridors where time's embraced,
Echoes wander, softly traced.
Thoughts reverberate, clear and still,
In the echoes, time stands still.
Moments from the past draw near,
Whisper secrets, soft and clear.
Timeless echoes of what's been,
In the chambers where they've been.
As time moves on, echoes stay,
In the heart of night and day.
Every whisper from the past,
Gives the present depth to cast.
Echoes form a melody,
A timeless song of memory.
In the echoes' gentle call,
Thoughts forever rise and fall.
As the echoes softly play,
They guide our thoughts in their way.
In the timeless, endless song,
Thoughts and memories belong.

50. The Boundless Horizon

Horizons stretch beyond our view,
In the mind's vast sky of blue.
Thoughts are wings that span the air,
Soaring where dreams dare to fare.
Every dawn brings fresh new light,
In the endless, boundless flight.
Horizons shift and ever grow,
In the realms where thoughts do flow.
No boundaries confine the dreams,
In the sky where starlight gleams.
Horizons wide, horizons grand,
In the spaces where thoughts expand.
As the sun sets, stars ignite,
In the vastness of the night.
Thoughts stretch far beyond our sight,
In the boundless, endless flight.
Endless vistas, wild and free,
In the sky where thoughts can be.
Horizons stretch, thoughts intertwine,
In the endless, boundless line.

EPHEMERAL THOUGHTS

51. Fleeting Shadows

In twilight's hush, where shadows dance,
The whispers of the day's last trance,
Ephemeral thoughts like fleeting mist,
In twilight's grip, they twist and twist.
They waltz on edges, soft and light,
With evening's sigh, they take their flight,
Each thought a spark that fades away,
In the gentle kiss of coming day.
Their essence lingers, faint and frail,
Like whispers in a ghostly tale,
Elusive as the morning dew,
They vanish with the sun's debut.
In dreams, they weave a soft refrain,
Of moments brief, yet not in vain,
Their whispers leave a trace so thin,
Yet carry echoes deep within.
When night is gone and light returns,
Their memory within us burns,
In fleeting thoughts, our hearts do find,
The whispers of the transient mind.

52. The Breath of Dawn

At dawn, a breath of fleeting grace,
Ephemeral thoughts begin to race,
Like mist that hugs the morning's cheek,
So soft, so slight, so rare to seek.
In waking hours, their dance is brief,
A whisper caught, a wisp of leaf,
They flutter through the early light,
Then fade away, out of our sight.
Yet in their wake, a warmth remains,
A subtle touch of joy, of pains,
In every thought that slips away,
A moment's truth, a soft display.
These thoughts like morning's dew are born,
And with the sun, they're swiftly worn,
Yet in their brevity we see,
The beauty in their mystery.
For in their fleeting, transient grace,
We glimpse eternity's embrace,
Ephemeral, they softly gleam,
The fragile threads of waking dream.

53. Evaporating Echoes

Ephemeral echoes softly play,
In fleeting thoughts, they drift away,
Like ripples on a tranquil lake,
They shimmer, fade, and softly break.
A whispered word, a fleeting glance,
A moment caught in time's own dance,
These echoes of our transient mind,
Are gentle threads of ties that bind.
In every thought that swiftly goes,
A fleeting joy, a sorrow's pose,
Their essence lingers just enough,
To remind us that life's not so tough.
Yet in their evanescence lies,
A deeper truth we recognize,
That in the briefest of our years,
Are hidden dreams and tender fears.
For though they vanish with the breeze,
These echoes leave us with a peace,
In every fleeting thought we find,
The whisper of the endless mind.

54. The Fleeting Muse

A muse so fleeting in its grace,
It touches briefly, leaves no trace,
Ephemeral as the morning star,
It lights the dark from near to far.
In moments rare, its light will gleam,
Like shadows caught within a dream,
Yet soon it fades, a sigh, a breath,
Lost in the wake of time and death.
Yet in its wake, a spark remains,
A fleeting joy, a hint of gains,
It whispers secrets soft and bright,
That linger just beyond our sight.
These thoughts so brief, they touch the soul,
In fragments small, they make us whole,
Their transient beauty, fragile, pure,
Is what we seek, and what we cure.
Though fleeting as the dawn's first light,
They leave us with a sense of right,
In every fleeting thought we see,
The muse that shapes our destiny.

55. Fleeting Moments

In fleeting moments, time does sway,
Ephemeral thoughts like shadows play,
They drift on breezes, soft and slight,
And vanish with the coming night.
They weave through daylight's tender seams,
In fragile, transient, delicate dreams,
Each thought a breath, a fleeting kiss,
A whisper lost in boundless bliss.
Yet in their brief, elusive glow,
A deeper truth they seem to show,
That in the fleeting, we discern,
A wisdom only time can learn.
For moments passed are never gone,
They linger in the hearts they've won,
Ephemeral as a passing storm,
They shape the soul and keep it warm.
So cherish thoughts that swiftly wane,
For in their briefness lies a gain,
In every fleeting moment's touch,
We find the things that mean so much.

56. Echoes of the Breeze

Ephemeral thoughts like breezes flow,
Soft whispers in the evening glow,
They glide through space, so light, so free,
And leave their trace in memory.
In every gust, a fleeting sound,
A moment's truth that can't be bound,
They whisper secrets to the night,
And drift away with dawn's first light.
Yet in their gentle, fleeting grace,
We find a soft, embracing space,
A whisper of the world unseen,
In every thought, a gentle sheen.
Though fleeting as the clouds above,
Their essence is a silent love,
A touch that dances through the air,
A thought that's whispered, soft and rare.
For in each fleeting breeze's song,
We find a truth that's pure and strong,
In echoes of the transient mind,
A subtle peace, a joy to find.

57. The Briefest Glow

In the briefest glow of twilight's beam,
Ephemeral thoughts like fleeting dreams,
They flicker softly, then are gone,
Lost in the hues of a coming dawn.
They shimmer in the fading light,
And vanish with the passing night,
Yet in their glow, a warmth does stay,
A touch of night within the day.
Each fleeting thought a soft caress,
A whisper of life's tenderness,
They leave a trace upon the heart,
A fleeting touch, a fragile art.
In their brevity, a truth we find,
A glimpse into the transient mind,
For though they vanish with the night,
They leave us with a soft delight.
In every fleeting, transient gleam,
We find a sense of quiet dream,
The briefest glow, so soft and bright,
Holds echoes of the fading light.

58. Wisp of Twilight

A wisp of twilight, fleeting, frail,
Ephemeral thoughts that softly sail,
They drift on currents, light and free,
And whisper secrets to the sea.
In moments brief, their essence shows,
Like moonlight on the river flows,
They touch the soul with gentle grace,
Then vanish, leaving no embrace.
Yet in their fleeting, fragile dance,
We glimpse the world's ephemeral chance,
A touch of truth, a hint of light,
In every fleeting, fragile night.
For in their brief and transient play,
A deeper meaning seems to stay,
A whisper of what's yet to be,
In every thought's soft melody.
So cherish every wisp, so rare,
For in their fleeting beauty there,
We find a glimpse of something grand,
A touch of dreams, a soft command.

59. The Passing Glance

A passing glance, so swift, so slight,
Ephemeral thoughts in morning's light,
They flicker in the corner's edge,
And vanish like a fleeting pledge.
In every glance, a world unfolds,
A story brief, a truth untold,
Yet in their brevity, we find,
A mirror to the fleeting mind.
For though they pass with light's first gleam,
They leave a trace, a subtle beam,
A moment's joy, a hint of grace,
A whisper in the endless space.
These thoughts that pass in fleeting style,
Bring depth to every fleeting smile,
And in their swift and brief embrace,
We find a tender, fleeting grace.
So hold each passing thought with care,
For in their briefness, moments share,
The essence of what's pure and true,
In every glance, a world anew.

60. Whispers of the Moment

Whispers of the moment pass,
Ephemeral thoughts like shadows cast,
They flit on breezes, light and free,
And drift away like leaves from trees.
In every whisper, soft and slight,
A fleeting truth comes into light,
Yet soon it fades with time's own hand,
Lost in the shifting sands of land.
Yet in their brief, elusive flight,
We sense a deeper, hidden light,
A fleeting touch, a soft refrain,
That lingers just beyond the plain.
For though they vanish with the day,
They leave a warmth that tends to stay,
In every whisper's fleeting grace,
We find a touch of time and space.
So treasure whispers, soft and rare,
For in their briefness lies a care,
A moment's truth, a transient kiss,
A whisper of the fleeting bliss.

MYSTICAL THOUGHTS

61. The Veil of Night

When shadows fold into the night,
The stars emerge in quiet light,
A veil of dreams begins to weave,
In cosmic whispers, hearts believe.
The moon, a lantern in the dark,
Guides wandering souls with silver spark,
Each star a secret, faintly cast,
On dreams that float through spaces vast.
In silence deep, where shadows blend,
Mystical realms begin to mend,
Timeless echoes softly call,
In night's embrace, we lose and fall.
The cosmic dance of dark and light,
Paints the sky in hues of night,
Where dreams take flight on wings unseen,
And stars become the night's serene.
Awake, embrace the night's soft glow,
Where mystic thoughts and wonders flow,
In the silence, the soul will find,
The whispers of the night, refined.

62. The Enchanted Forest

In the forest, shadows play,
Where light and dark blend into day,
Ancient trees with wisdom's grace,
Whisper secrets in their space.
Among the ferns, where silence grows,
Mystic tales the wind bestows,
The mist reveals a hidden guide,
Through paths where faerie dreams abide.
Leaves murmur in the twilight air,
Of lands where magic lingers there,
In every rustle, soft and light,
Ancient stories take their flight.
The forest's breath is full of lore,
With echoes from an age before,
Through moonlit glades and shadowed glen,
The soul can wander, free from ken.
So tread with care the woodland's grace,
And let its magic interlace,
In every whisper, find a clue,
To realms where dreams and truths accrue.

63. The Celestial Dance

Stars align in cosmic sway,
In the velvet sky's grand ballet,
Galaxies in silent flight,
Weave their tales through endless night.
Celestial rhythms softly play,
Guiding dreams in their own way,
Planets spin in graceful arcs,
Guided by the universe's marks.
Nebulae in colors blend,
As time and space together mend,
A tapestry of light divine,
In the cosmos' grand design.
Each twinkle tells of distant lands,
Of ancient myths and stellar strands,
In the vast expanse, dreams find space,
In the dance of stars and grace.
So let the cosmic dance unfold,
In starlit tales and wonders bold,
The universe, with its endless show,
Guides the soul where dreams can grow.

64. The Moonlit Lake

Underneath the moon's soft light,
The lake reflects a silver night,
Ripples dance in gentle grace,
Echoes of a dream's embrace.
Stars descend to kiss the tide,
In the water's depths, secrets hide,
A mirror to the night's soft sheen,
Where dreams and shadows intermingle, keen.
The moon's embrace is tender, true,
Casting light in shades of blue,
The lake holds whispers of the past,
In its calm, the moments last.
Twilight weaves its gentle shroud,
Mystic dreams are softly vowed,
In the lake's serene, still expanse,
The soul finds space to drift and dance.
So let your thoughts on water glide,
In moonlight's magic, let them bide,
The lake reflects what dreams unfold,
In its depths, mysteries told.

65. The Wandering Star

A star that wanders through the night,
Guides the heart with distant light,
Across the sky's dark, endless sea,
It sails on waves of mystery.
Its path a secret, veiled and grand,
A journey through the cosmic land,
In realms where time and dreams entwine,
And stardust weaves the night's design.
Each twinkle speaks of worlds afar,
Where dreams are born and visions are,
In its light, the soul finds grace,
A beacon in the darkened space.
As dawn approaches, light will fade,
Yet in its wake, a thought is laid,
A spark of wonder, softly bright,
In the wandering star's soft light.
So follow where the star may lead,
Through realms where mystic dreams succeed,
In its glow, the heart finds home,
On cosmic paths where dreams may roam.

66. The Timeless Whisper

In realms where time and space dissolve,
Timeless whispers gently solve,
The mysteries that shadows weave,
In echoes, the heart can believe.
Voices from the ancient past,
In shadows, secrets softly cast,
Their murmurs blend with space and time,
In melodies, so soft, so prime.
Each whisper holds a truth so clear,
Of ages old and futures near,
In fleeting moments, wisdom calls,
From ancient echoes through the halls.
In stillness, timeless wisdom sings,
Of dreams and truths and cosmic things,
Through ages long and moments bright,
The whispers bring the heart to light.
So listen close to echoes rare,
In timeless whispers, find the fare,
Where dreams and truths in silence meet,
In realms where time and thought are sweet.

67. The Eternal Flame

In the heart of night's embrace,
Burns a flame with gentle grace,
A beacon through the darkened sea,
Of dreams and thoughts that wander free.
The fire's dance, both fierce and mild,
Illuminates the mystic wild,
Its light a bridge to realms unknown,
Where dreams and visions gently hone.
Each flicker tells a tale so grand,
Of legends lost and magic planned,
In its warmth, the spirit finds,
A path where thought and dream entwine.
In the flame's eternal light,
The soul's true journey comes to sight,
A pilgrimage through realms unseen,
Where dreams and thoughts are softly gleaned.
So let the flame guide you afar,
Through mystic realms and dreams bizarre,
In its light, find truth and grace,
The eternal fire's warm embrace.

68. The Dreamweaver's Spell

In twilight's gentle, rare embrace,
The dreamweaver weaves her lace,
With threads of starlight, moonlight's hue,
She casts a spell of visions true.
Each thread a whisper, soft and faint,
Of dreams that blend and spirits paint,
In hues of twilight's tender shade,
Where dreams and magic softly wade.
Her loom of stars and moonlit night,
Spins patterns of ethereal light,
She weaves the threads of sleep and grace,
In dreams that time cannot erase.
As dawn approaches, spell will fade,
Yet in the night's enchanted glade,
The dreams she wove shall softly rest,
In the heart of every quest.
So let the dreamweaver's spell unfold,
In twilight's magic, stories told,
Where visions dance and dreams arise,
In the night's gentle, mystic guise.

69. The Oracle's Vision

In the chamber of the seer's gaze,
Where shadows blend with mystic haze,
The oracle reveals the truth,
In visions of both age and youth.
Her eyes, a mirror to the soul,
Show paths where dreams and fate unroll,
Through realms where time and space entwine,
And futures in the past align.
With whispers from the cosmic sea,
She charts the course of destiny,
In realms where dreams and visions blend,
And timeless truths around us wend.
The future and the past collide,
In her visions, secrets bide,
Each glance a journey through the veils,
Where fate and dreams in silence sail.
So seek the oracle's soft light,
In visions where the heart takes flight,
The paths she shows are clear and bright,
In realms where truth and dreams unite.

70. The Hidden Realm

Beyond the veil of mortal sight,
A hidden realm lies soft and bright,
Where dreams and magic intertwine,
In places where the stars align.
In silence deep and shadowed space,
Mysteries of the soul embrace,
The hidden realm where thoughts take flight,
And ancient echoes softly light.
The air is filled with mystic song,
Where timeless echoes drift along,
In every whisper, magic stirs,
And dreams in silence gently purr.
The hidden realm's a sacred place,
Where time and dreams and thoughts embrace,
In its depths, the soul may find,
A path where wonders are defined.
So enter where the hidden lies,
In realms where dreams and mystic rise,
The heart shall wander, ever free,
In the hidden realm of mystery.

REFLECTIVE THOUGHTS

71. The Mirror of Dawn

At dawn's first light, the world awakes,
The mirror of the morning breaks,
Each ray reflects a day anew,
Where thoughts and dreams begin to brew.
In shadows cast by morning's grace,
We find the truth within the space,
The past and future softly blend,
In dawn's embrace, they intertwine and mend.
The light reveals what night conceals,
In quiet moments, truth reveals,
The heart reflects on paths once trod,
In dawn's soft glow, the soul finds God.
The day unfolds with gentle hands,
As moments shift like drifting sands,
Each hour brings a chance to see,
The deeper truths that set us free.
So greet the day with open eyes,
In morning's light, let wisdom rise,
For in each dawn, a chance to find,
The reflections of a thoughtful mind.

72. The Passage of Time

Time flows like a river's stream,
Winding through our hopes and dreams,
Each moment shapes the days we see,
In time's embrace, we find our plea.
The past, a shadow in our wake,
The future, paths that we will take,
In every tick of the clock's hand,
We find the marks where we have planned.
The present holds the key to peace,
Where time and thoughts in stillness cease,
In every second's fleeting grace,
We glimpse the soul's own hidden space.
The hours pass, but lessons stay,
In every dawn, in every day,
Reflecting on the moments gone,
We find our place as time moves on.
So cherish each moment's gentle flow,
For in its current, truths will show,
The passage of time, a sacred guide,
In every day, where dreams reside.

73. The Silent Reflection

In the stillness of the night,
Thoughts emerge in soft twilight,
The heart reflects in silence deep,
Where secrets of the soul may seep.
In quiet hours, the mind takes flight,
Unraveling the truths of night,
The world outside begins to fade,
In silent thoughts, our fears are laid.
The moonlight casts a gentle hue,
On every dream and every view,
In silence, we find solace clear,
Where whispered thoughts are always near.
The stars above, a distant light,
Guide the soul through the tranquil night,
In moments still, reflections blend,
In silent depths, we start to mend.
So let the night's soft silence bring,
The calm where hidden thoughts can sing,
In quiet hours, find peace of mind,
And in reflection, truth unwind.

74. The Path of Reflection

Life's path is lined with thoughts so grand,
Reflecting on the shifting sand,
Each step we take reveals a view,
Of dreams and memories we pursue.
In every choice, in every turn,
The heart reflects on what we yearn,
The journey's length, the moments wide,
In every path, our truths abide.
The road ahead is not so clear,
Yet in reflection, we draw near,
To understand the lessons learned,
In every step, where hopes are burned.
The past and future softly blend,
In every twist and every bend,
We trace our steps and find our way,
In reflection, night and day.
So walk the path with mindful gaze,
In every turn, through life's maze,
Reflect on where the journey goes,
And find the truth in each repose.

75. The Whisper of Wisdom

In the stillness of the mind,
Wisdom's whispers we can find,
Softly spoken, truth reveals,
In gentle words, the heart heals.
The lessons learned, both near and far,
Illuminate like a guiding star,
In wisdom's light, the soul will see,
The path to its own clarity.
Through reflective thoughts and quiet grace,
We find the truths that time has traced,
In every whisper, soft and wise,
We glimpse the soul's own clear sunrise.
The heart, in silence, hears the call,
Of wisdom's voice that guides us all,
In gentle tones and truths we find,
A mirror to the peaceful mind.
So listen close to wisdom's plea,
In every thought, in every sea,
For in the whispers, soft and bright,
The soul finds guidance, clear and right.

76. The Rhythm of Reflection

The rhythm of our thoughts unfolds,
In patterns soft and stories told,
Each beat a moment, sharp and clear,
Reflecting what we hold dear.
The heart's own cadence, soft and slow,
Reveals the paths we choose to go,
In rhythm, truths emerge anew,
As memories and dreams come through.
In every pulse, a lesson lies,
A beat of time where wisdom flies,
The rhythm of reflection beats,
In harmony with life's own feats.
The soul finds rhythm in its quest,
In every thought, in every test,
Reflective beats that gently guide,
Through moments of both dark and bright.
So follow where the rhythm leads,
In every thought, in every deed,
For in the beats of heart and mind,
Reflection's rhythm, peace will find.

77. The Echo of Memory

In memory's hall, the echoes play,
Reflecting on the passing day,
The moments linger, soft and clear,
In every thought, the past is near.
The echoes tell of joys and pain,
Of moments lost and dreams gained,
In every sound, a story stays,
In memory's deep, reflective ways.
The past may drift, but echoes remain,
A soundtrack to our joy and pain,
In every whisper, soft and light,
The echoes of the past take flight.
The heart revisits what's long gone,
In echoes that live on and on,
Reflecting on the life we lead,
In every sound, a thought we heed.
So cherish the echoes of the past,
In every memory, truth is cast,
For in the echoes, we find grace,
And reflect on time's enduring space.

78. The Light of Insight

Insight dawns like morning's light,
Illuminating shadows bright,
In every thought, a spark ignites,
Revealing truths in purest sights.
The light of insight gently warms,
Guiding through life's shifting forms,
In clarity, the soul perceives,
The wisdom that the heart believes.
In every beam, a truth appears,
Dispelling doubts and silent fears,
The light reveals what's often missed,
In every thought, the soul persists.
The dawn of insight clears the haze,
In every light, a thoughtful gaze,
Reflecting on what lies ahead,
With clarity, our paths are spread.
So embrace the light of insight's grace,
In every dawn, find your own place,
For in the clarity it brings,
The soul discovers deeper things.

79. The Stillness of Truth

In stillness, truth begins to bloom,
Dispelling shadows, clearing gloom,
The heart reflects in quiet grace,
Where truth reveals its gentle face.
The silence holds the deepest thoughts,
In stillness, clarity is brought,
The mind finds peace in calm's embrace,
In truth's own light, we find our place.
The world may rush, but stillness stays,
A refuge in the hectic maze,
Where truth and wisdom gently flow,
In quiet moments, we bestow.
The soul finds solace in the calm,
In stillness, we can find the balm,
To heal and guide, to understand,
The truths that lie at life's own hand.
So seek the stillness, find the peace,
In quiet moments, thoughts release,
For in the stillness, truth is found,
And wisdom's voice is ever sound.

80. The Horizon of Thought

The horizon stretches wide and far,
A canvas where our thoughts are starred,
In every line and every view,
Reflective dreams come into view.
The edge of thought meets endless sky,
Where hopes and visions gently lie,
In the distance, truths unfold,
In horizons bright and bold.
The journey's length is yet unknown,
In every step, new seeds are sown,
The horizon guides with distant light,
Reflecting paths of day and night.
The heart can see beyond the far,
To dreams and thoughts that gently spar,
In every view, the soul will find,
Horizons where the heart is kind.
So gaze upon the distant line,
In horizons bright, let thoughts align,
For in the view, reflections clear,
Reveal the dreams we hold so dear.

HIDDEN THOUGHTS

81. The Secret Whisper

In quiet corners of the mind,
Hidden thoughts are softly twined,
In whispers low, they softly play,
Where shadows dance and dreams hold sway.
The heart conceals what words can't share,
In silent depths, thoughts softly fare,
The hidden truths, in silence kept,
In corners where the soul has slept.
Each fleeting thought, a secret spun,
In quiet moments, one by one,
Reveals a glimpse of what's concealed,
In hidden depths, truths are revealed.
The mind's own veil, a gentle shield,
Where hidden dreams and thoughts are healed,
In whispers soft and shadows deep,
The heart's own secrets gently seep.
So listen close to silence' call,
Where hidden thoughts and shadows fall,
In every whisper, truth will find,
A path to what lies in the mind.

82. The Veiled Mirror

In the mirror's hidden frame,
Thoughts reflect but not the same,
A veiled image softly shows,
Where secret dreams and shadows pose.
Behind the glass, the truth is blurred,
In silent echoes, whispers heard,
The mirror holds what light obscures,
In veiled reflections, truth endures.
The heart's own image softly veils,
In every glance, the truth unveils,
A hidden world that lies within,
Where thoughts and dreams begin to spin.
In gentle hues and shadows cast,
The mirrored thoughts from present, past,
Reflect the secrets we conceal,
In veiled reflections, truths reveal.
So gaze into the mirror's light,
Where hidden thoughts come into sight,
In every veiled and whispered grace,
The heart's true secrets find their place.

83. The Silent Chamber

In the chamber of the soul,
Hidden thoughts take soft control,
In silence deep, they softly wait,
Behind the door of heart's own gate.
Each hidden dream and silent plea,
In chambers locked, is known to me,
The heart's own secrets softly lie,
In quiet depths where shadows sigh.
The chamber's silence, soft and clear,
Holds the thoughts we seldom hear,
In every echo, truth will find,
A hidden realm within the mind.
The heart reveals what words can't say,
In chambers where the secrets stay,
In stillness where the thoughts take flight,
The soul finds solace in the night.
So enter deep where shadows dwell,
In silent chambers, truth will tell,
For in the heart's own hidden space,
The soul finds its reflective place.

84. The Secret Garden

In the garden of the mind,
Hidden thoughts are gently lined,
Where flowers bloom in secret hues,
And silent dreams are softly used.
In every petal, truths unfold,
In hidden corners, dreams are bold,
The garden keeps the heart's own lore,
In secret blooms and shadows' store.
The mind's own garden, lush and deep,
Where hidden thoughts and dreams do sleep,
In every leaf and flower's grace,
The heart reveals its hidden space.
Through whispered winds and gentle rain,
The garden holds the heart's refrain,
In silent growth and subtle grace,
The soul's own secrets find their place.
So tend the garden, pure and bright,
Where hidden thoughts come to the light,
In every bloom and shaded path,
The heart finds peace in quiet wrath.

85. The Cloak of Dreams

In the cloak of twilight's hue,
Hidden dreams and thoughts accrue,
In every fold and shadowed seam,
The heart's own secrets softly gleam.
The cloak conceals what day might show,
In whispered tones, the dreams will flow,
The heart's own wishes wrapped in light,
In hidden depths, away from sight.
Each fold of cloak holds thoughts concealed,
In twilight's veil, the truth revealed,
The dreams we keep in secret's grace,
In shadows' fold, we find our place.
The cloak of night, a gentle shield,
Where hidden dreams and truths are healed,
In softest folds and whispered streams,
The heart reflects its hidden dreams.
So wear the cloak with tender care,
In every fold, find dreams laid bare,
For in the hidden, gentle light,
The heart's own secrets take their flight.

86. The Hall Of Echoes

In the hall where echoes play,
Hidden thoughts begin to sway,
In every sound and gentle beat,
The heart's own secrets softly meet.
The echoes tell of what is masked,
In shadows where the truths are tasked,
Each reverberation softly brings,
The hidden thoughts and secret things.
The hall's own whispers softly drift,
In every echo, truths uplift,
The mind reflects in sound's embrace,
Where hidden dreams and thoughts find space.
In silent echoes, heart reveals,
What daylight's glare may never seal,
The echoes of the soul's own plight,
In hidden halls, come to light.
So listen to the echoes near,
In every sound, find what is clear,
For in the hall where secrets call,
The heart's own truths will softly fall.

87. The Hidden Depths

In the depths where shadows dwell,
Hidden thoughts are hard to tell,
In every quiet, gentle wave,
The heart's own secrets softly crave.
The depths conceal what light may miss,
In silent realms, the thoughts find bliss,
In every whisper of the deep,
The heart's own secrets softly seep.
The mind's own depths, a hidden sea,
Where thoughts and dreams are wild and free,
In every current, truth is spun,
In silent depths, the heart's begun.
The darkness holds what day can't see,
In hidden realms of secrecy,
In depths where silent shadows roam,
The heart finds truths that feel like home.
So dive into the depths with care,
Where hidden thoughts and dreams are fair,
In every wave and silent deep,
The heart's own secrets softly seep.

88. The Hidden Lullaby

In the lullaby of night's embrace,
Hidden thoughts find their own place,
In gentle tones and softest sighs,
The heart's own secrets softly rise.
The lullaby, a soothing sound,
In hidden realms where thoughts are bound,
In every note and gentle strain,
The dreams and truths are soft and plain.
The night's own song, a tender guide,
Where hidden dreams and thoughts reside,
In lullabies of dark and light,
The heart finds peace in quiet flight.
The soothing melody will bring,
The hidden truths on softly wing,
In every note, the heart's own song,
In lullabies where dreams belong.
So listen to the night's soft hum,
Where hidden thoughts and dreams are spun,
For in the lullaby of night,
The heart's own secrets come to light.

89. The Secret Path

On the path where shadows blend,
Hidden thoughts and dreams ascend,
In quiet steps and silent tread,
The heart's own secrets softly spread.
The path may twist and turn away,
But hidden thoughts are here to stay,
In every curve and gentle bend,
The heart reveals its secret friend.
In every footfall, truths are known,
In quiet steps, the dreams are sown,
The path of shadows holds the key,
To hidden realms where hearts are free.
The journey's length may seem unclear,
But hidden thoughts are always near,
In every step and silent trace,
The heart's own secrets find their place.
So walk the path with gentle grace,
Where hidden thoughts and dreams embrace,
In every step and silent plea,
The heart finds peace and mystery.

90. The Hidden Symphony

In the symphony of night's own tone,
Hidden thoughts are softly shown,
In every note and gentle sound,
The heart's own secrets can be found.
The music plays in shadows deep,
Where hidden dreams and thoughts will sleep,
In every chord and quiet pause,
The heart reveals its silent cause.
The symphony of night will bring,
The hidden truths on gentle wing,
In every melody and beat,
The dreams and thoughts find their retreat.
In every note, a story's told,
In symphonies where secrets hold,
The heart's own song will softly rise,
In hidden realms where truth lies.
So listen to the night's own song,
Where hidden thoughts and dreams belong,
For in the symphony's embrace,
The heart's true secrets find their place.

COSMIC THOUGHTS

91. The Starlit Reverie

Beneath the vast, celestial dome,
Where distant stars and comets roam,
The cosmos whispers in the night,
A tale of stars, of dark and light.
Galaxies twirl in cosmic dance,
In silken threads of fate and chance,
Each twinkle writes a fleeting dream,
In endless space, where thoughts will gleam.
The nebulae in hues so bright,
Reflect the thoughts of endless night,
The universe, a canvas wide,
Where cosmic musings gently glide.
Amongst the stars, where silence reigns,
The soul's own echoes drift like chains,
In cosmic currents, truths unwind,
In every star, a thought aligned.
So gaze into the velvet sky,
Where cosmic whispers softly fly,
For in the night's vast, endless fold,
The heart's own thoughts are bright and bold.

92. Celestial Secrets

In cosmic depths, where shadows play,
Celestial secrets find their way,
The stars, they hold a silent lore,
Of endless realms and ancient more.
Galaxies spin their tales in gold,
In cosmic winds, their truths unfold,
The constellations write in fire,
Of dreams and hopes that never tire.
Each planet's path, a silent guide,
Through cosmic seas, the thoughts will ride,
In every orbit, every beam,
Lie cosmic truths and stardust dreams.
The universe, a grand design,
In cosmic dance, the stars align,
In whispered winds of space so deep,
The heart's own thoughts are sown and reap.
So listen to the cosmic call,
Where celestial secrets softly fall,
For in the vast, eternal light,
The soul's own thoughts take cosmic flight.

93. The Cosmic Tapestry

In the tapestry of night so grand,
The cosmos weaves with gentle hand,
Stars are threads of silver bright,
In the fabric of the endless night.
Nebulae like bursts of flame,
Embroider thoughts in astral claim,
The universe, a woven seam,
Where cosmic musings softly dream.
In every constellation's trace,
The heart finds patterns, stars embrace,
Galaxies spin their silent tales,
In cosmic rhythm, thought prevails.
The tapestry of space unfolds,
In starlit strands and colors bold,
In every star and cosmic hue,
The soul's own whispers find their cue.
So ponder deep the cosmic weave,
In every star and thread, believe,
For in the night's grand, endless scheme,
The heart's own thoughts are woven dream.

94. The Astral Symphony

In the symphony of cosmic sound,
Where distant stars and planets bound,
The universe sings in tones so pure,
A melody that will endure.
Galaxies hum a gentle tune,
In rhythms bright as summer's moon,
The heart's own song joins cosmic play,
In melodies of night and day.
The asteroids and comets dance,
In harmony and fleeting chance,
Their orbits write a song of grace,
In stellar notes through boundless space.
In every star's and planet's breath,
A cosmic music stirs from death,
The soul's own rhythms blend with light,
In symphonies of endless night.
So listen to the astral choir,
Where cosmic thoughts and dreams aspire,
For in the night's melodious stream,
The heart's own thoughts are like a dream.

95. The Galactic Dream

In the dreamscape of the galaxy,
Where cosmic thoughts roam wild and free,
The stars paint visions in the night,
Of dreams and hopes in endless flight.
Nebulae swirl in colors bright,
In cosmic dreams of starry light,
Each constellation softly beams,
A guide to stardust-laden dreams.
The Milky Way's a river wide,
Where cosmic thoughts and dreams reside,
In every star and comet's tail,
The heart's own dreams set sail and sail.
In galaxies where shadows blend,
The soul's own wishes softly mend,
Among the stars, where dreams are spun,
The heart's own cosmic thoughts are one.
So drift upon the galactic stream,
Where cosmic thoughts and dreams redeem,
In every star's and planet's gleam,
The heart finds peace in cosmic dream.

96. The Cosmic Tide

In the cosmic tide of night,
Where galaxies and stars ignite,
The universe flows in silent grace,
A boundless sea of endless space.
The nebulae in colors blend,
In cosmic waves that never end,
The heart's own thoughts, like tides, will rise,
In endless dance beneath the skies.
The planets drift in rhythmic sweep,
Their orbits in the darkness deep,
The cosmic sea, a vast expanse,
Where thoughts and dreams in silence dance.
In stardust trails and comet's flight,
The heart's own dreams find boundless light,
In every wave of cosmic sea,
The soul finds solace wild and free.
So ride the tide of night with care,
Where cosmic dreams and thoughts declare,
In every wave and starry sweep,
The heart's own secrets softly sleep.

97. The Nebula's Embrace

In the nebula's soft embrace,
Where stardust dreams and thoughts find place,
The universe breathes out in light,
A cosmic glow that warms the night.
Nebulae in hues so grand,
Wrap the stars with gentle hand,
In every swirl and cloud of fire,
The heart's own thoughts find deep desire.
The cosmic dust in silence spreads,
In astral fields and stardust beds,
The nebula's embrace will guide,
The soul through cosmic waves so wide.
In every star and cosmic mist,
The heart finds dreams that softly twist,
In nebula's tender, glowing grace,
The heart's own thoughts find their own space.
So feel the nebula's warm embrace,
In every star and cosmic space,
For in the night's celestial glow,
The heart's own dreams begin to flow.

98. The Celestial Canvas

On the celestial canvas wide,
Where stars and galaxies reside,
The universe paints with cosmic brush,
A masterpiece of silent hush.
Galaxies swirl in colors grand,
In cosmic art across the land,
The heart reflects the stars' own grace,
In every stroke, a dream's embrace.
The constellations sketch their tale,
In stellar patterns that unveil,
The universe, a canvas deep,
Where cosmic thoughts and dreams will sleep.
In every star and nebula's hue,
The heart finds art that feels so true,
On cosmic canvas, thoughts are bright,
In every shade of dark and light.
So gaze upon the celestial art,
Where cosmic dreams and thoughts depart,
For in the universe's grand design,
The heart's own visions intertwine.

99. The Starry Path

On the starry path so bright,
Where cosmic thoughts and dreams take flight,
The stars illuminate the way,
To realms where hidden dreams can play.
The constellations mark the route,
In cosmic maps where dreams are moot,
The heart's own journey through the night,
Is guided by the starry light.
The Milky Way's a trail of dreams,
In cosmic threads and stardust beams,
The soul will follow, step by step,
In pathways where the thoughts are kept.
In every star and galaxy,
The heart finds dreams of destiny,
On the starry path, the soul will tread,
In cosmic light where dreams are led.
So walk the path with stars in sight,
Where cosmic thoughts and dreams unite,
For in the night's own guiding light,
The heart's true path will shine so bright.

100. The Universe's Heartbeat

In the universe's gentle beat,
Where cosmic rhythms softly meet,
The stars and planets pulse in time,
To the heart's own cosmic rhyme.
The galaxies in swirling grace,
Keep the rhythm of the space,
In every pulse and silent thrum,
The heart and cosmos gently hum.
The universe, a grand design,
In every beat, the stars align,
The cosmic rhythm guides the soul,
In every heartbeat, thoughts unfold.
In stardust trails and celestial song,
The heart finds where it does belong,
In cosmic beats and starry light,
The soul's own rhythm takes its flight.
So feel the universe's beat,
Where cosmic thoughts and dreams will meet,
For in the rhythm of the night,
The heart finds peace and pure delight.

THE END

As you close the final pages of "**Thoughts: Whispers of the Soul**," may you carry with you the **echoes** of these **reflections** and **dreams**. Each poem is a fragment of the **human experience**, a **whisper** from the depths of our **collective soul**, inviting you to **explore** the intimate **landscapes of emotion and thought**. I hope these words have **resonated** with you, offering **solace, inspiration**, or simply a **moment of quiet contemplation**. Thank you for joining me on this journey through the **delicate art of poetry**, where each whisper is a **testament** to the beauty found in our **shared humanity**.

- THANK YOU -

www.ingramcontent.com/pod-product-compliance
Lightning Source LLC
La Vergne TN
LVHW041102150826
845673LV00007B/1893

* 9 7 9 8 8 9 5 5 6 5 9 0 2 *